to...

with love

from...

A & W Publishers, Inc.
New York

First published in the United States of America in
1980 by A & W Publishers, Inc.,
95 Madison Avenue, New York, New York 10016.
By arrangement with Weidenfeld & Nicolson Ltd.

Library of Congress Catalog Card Number: 80-7822
ISBN: 0-89479-069-2

Printed in Italy by L.E.G.O., Vicenza.

Foreword

The 'lipograph' was the inspired, if bizarre, invention of international pop star David Bowie. In London for a concert, he was presented with a box of cosmetics by Charles of the Ritz and, to thank them, he sent in return a print of his lips – made with lipstick on a card. So many people wanted to buy the lip print that a highly original idea was born – an auction of lipographs to raise money for charity. World-famous personalities were asked to put painted lips to paper, and an auction was held at Sotheby's in 1979, the Year of the Child, in aid of the Save the Children Fund who were celebrating their Diamond Jubilee. With all the solemnity usually bestowed on an auction of fine art, Sotheby's sold the entire collection, the lipograph of Mick Jagger fetching the highest price of £800.

This ingenious and very successful idea has now been extended to a book. Many of the lipographs from the auction are reproduced on the following pages, and a number of others have been specially acquired. All royalties from publication will go to Save the Children, augmenting the proceeds of the auction and so providing continued support for the projects of the cause.

5

Contents

48 Amanda Lear
49 Lord Lichfield
50 Sophia Loren
51 Joanna Lumley
52 Kenneth MacMillan
53 The Duchess
   of Marlborough
54 Malcolm McDowell
55 Ian McKellen
56 Hayley Mills
57 Warren Mitchell
58 Marian Montgomery
59 Nanette Newman

60 Olivia Newton-John
61 Jack Nicholson
62 David Niven
63 Michael Parkinson
64 Luciano Pavarotti
65 Robert Powell
66 Mary Quant
67 Christopher Reeve
68 Cliff Richard
69 Leonard Rossiter
70 Omar Sharif
71 Gerald Scarfe
72 Terence Stamp

73 Elaine Stritch
74 Elizabeth Taylor
75 John Travolta
76 The Three Degrees
77 Peter Ustinov
78 Dennis Waterman
79 Mae West
80 Michael York

Acknowledgements

Thanks from Save the Children
SAVE THE CHILDREN is Britain's largest international children's charity. It is wholly concerned with the rescue and long-term welfare of children in hunger, sickness and need, irrespective of country, nationality, race or religion. After the auction at Sotheby's of celebrity lip prints we discovered that a lipograph is a very successful fundraiser. It's also one of those inspired ideas which appeals to the press and generates a lot of valuable publicity for us. We are most grateful to Charles of the Ritz for sponsoring the event, and particularly to Felicity Bosanquet for having the idea and for working so hard to make it a success.

THE PUBLISHERS would like to acknowledge the following, who kindly lent us the lipographs they acquired through the Sotheby's auction: Patrick Gwynn-Jones of Pomegranates Restaurant for the lipographs of David Essex and Gerald Harper; 'Kitty' for the lipograph of Barbara Cartland; Percy Savage of Fashion Promotions Ltd for the lipographs of Lyndall Hobbs and Angelica Huston; Bruce Oldfield for the lipograph of Luciano Pavarotti.

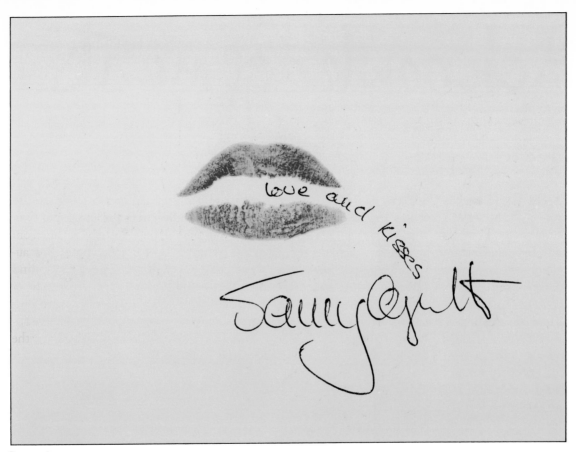

love and kisses

Jenny Agutter

June - 2 - 19 - 79

Love is the net
where Hearts are
Caught like fish

Muhammad Ali
Three time Campion of
Boxing World.

a Gem to the
World

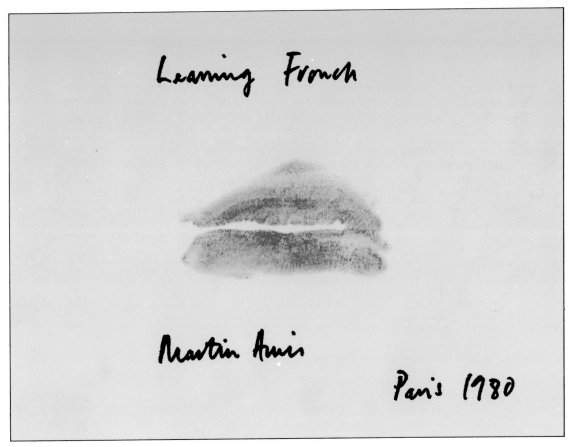

Learning French

Martin Amis

Paris 1980

Martin Amis

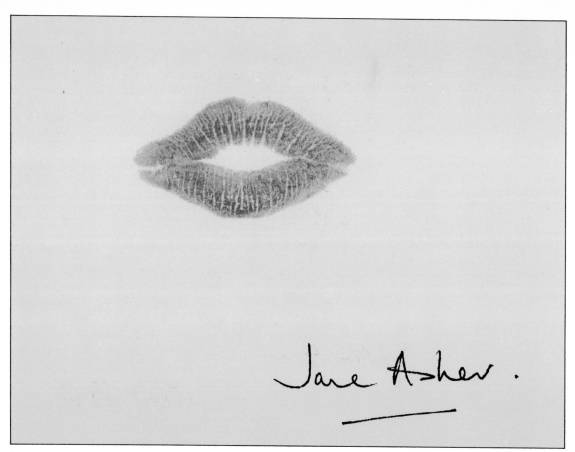

12   Jane Asher

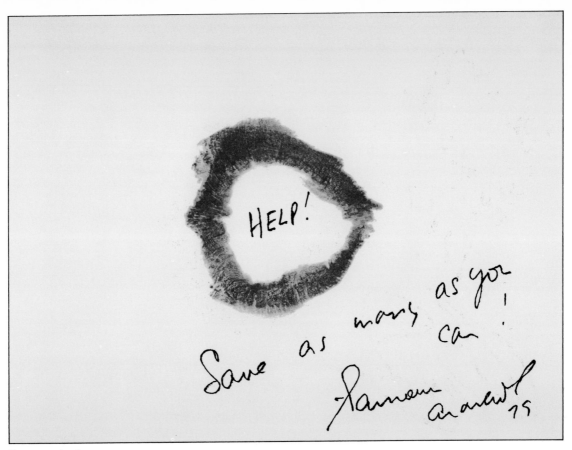

Eamonn Andrews

14   David Bailey

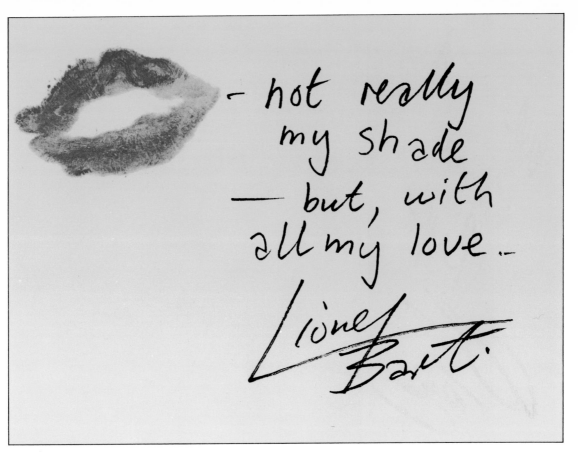

— not really
my shade
— but, with
all my love —

Lionel
Bart.

All Good Things
in the New Year —

Candice
Bergen

16   Candice Bergen

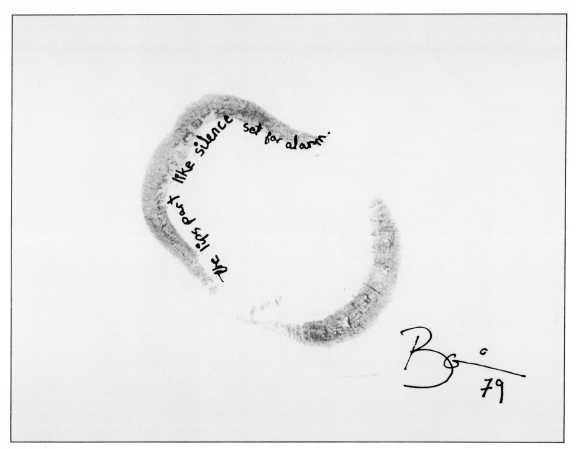

the 'sick part' like silence set for alarm.

David Bowie

17

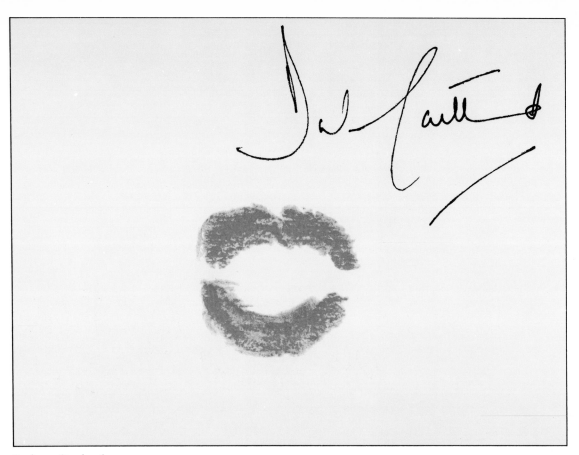

Barbara Cartland

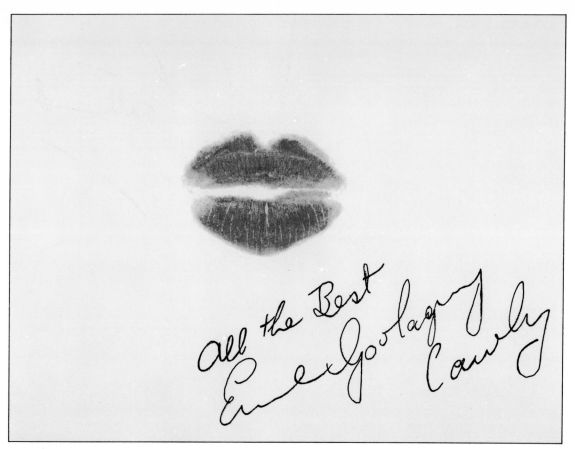

All the Best
Evonne Goolagong Cawley

Evonne Cawley

Christopher Cazenove

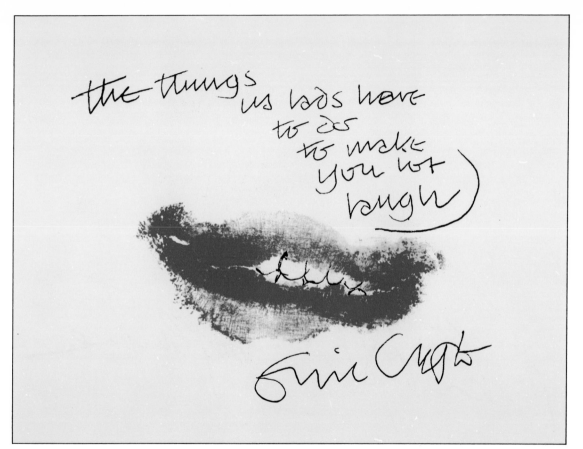

the things us lads have
to do
to make
you not
laugh)

Eric Clapton

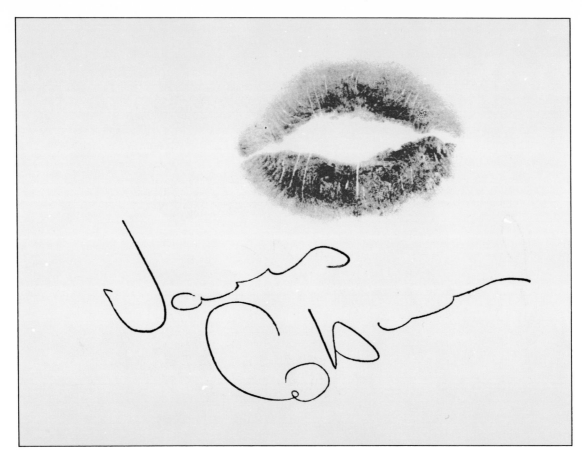

James Coburn

Joan Collins

love and One Kiss

from *JCleese*

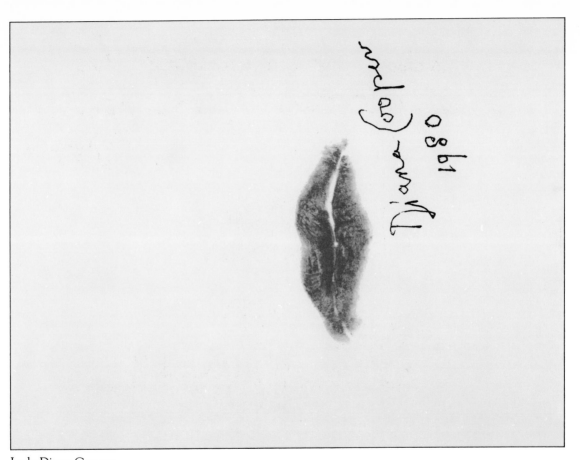

Lady Diana Cooper

excuse the smudge, its
my first time (with a piece...
                 of paper)

Sean Connery

Sean Connery

just a teaser!

John Dankworth

John Dankworth

27

28   Bette Davis

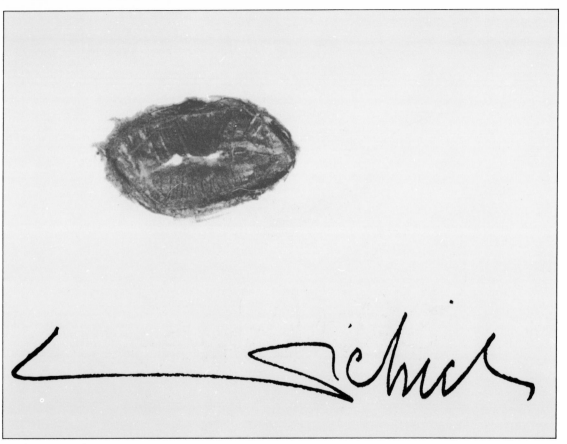

Marlene Dietrich

Placido Domingo

Virgin Kisses! Almost!

With my best wishes!
Kirk Douglas

Kirk Douglas

31

love
Lesley Anne Down

Lesley-Anne Down

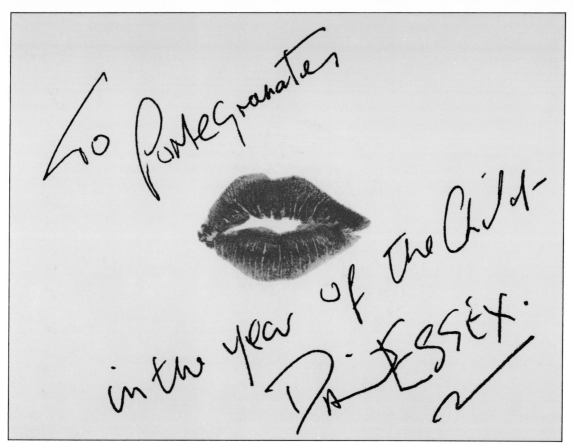

To Pomegranates

in the year of the Child—

D. ESSEX.

David Essex

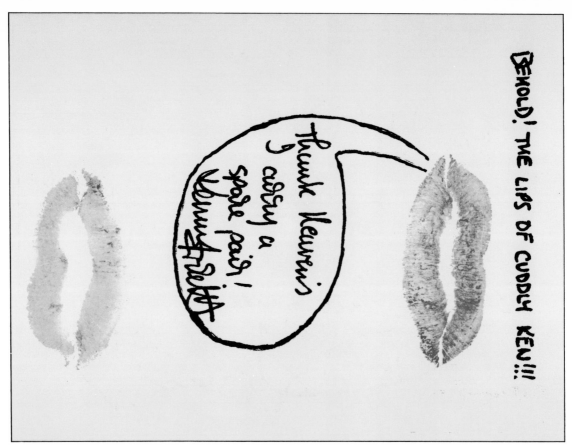

Kenny Everett

With best wishes,
Farrah 79

Farrah Fawcett

Douglas Fairbanks

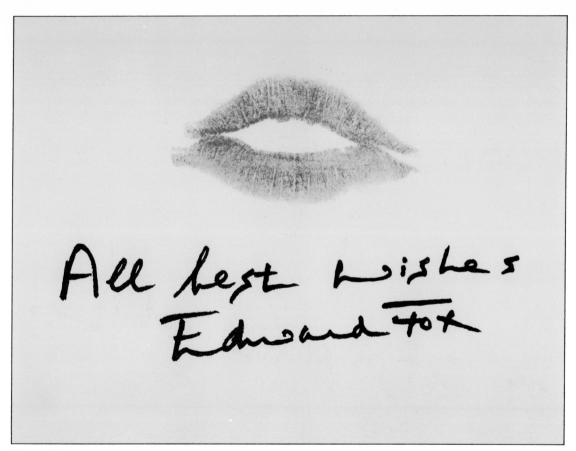

Edward Fox

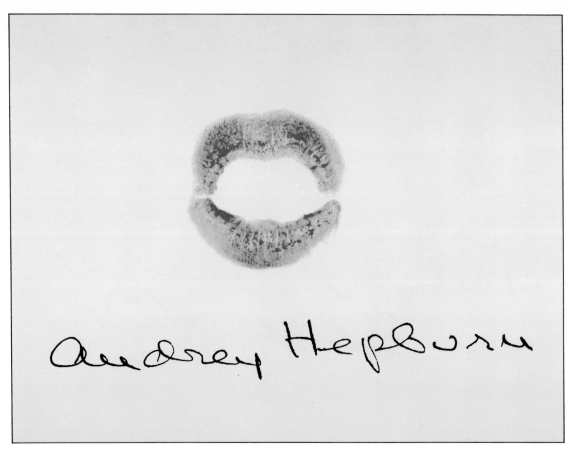

Audrey Hepburn

Lyndall Hobbs

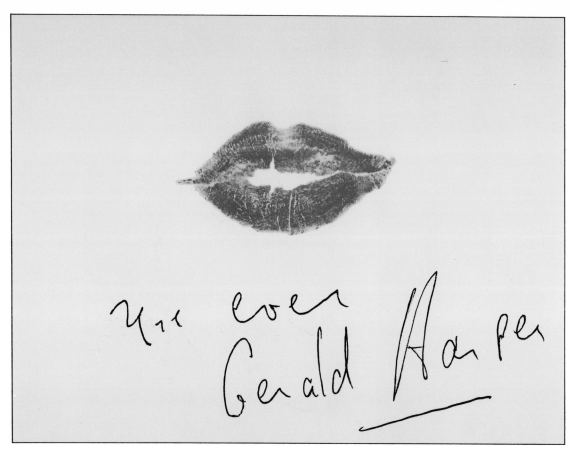

Yrr ever
Gerald Harper

40   Gerald Harper

Gayle Hunnicutt

42   James Hunt

Angelica Huston

With love & best wishes ————

Gordon Jackson

Gordon Jackson

Mick Jagger

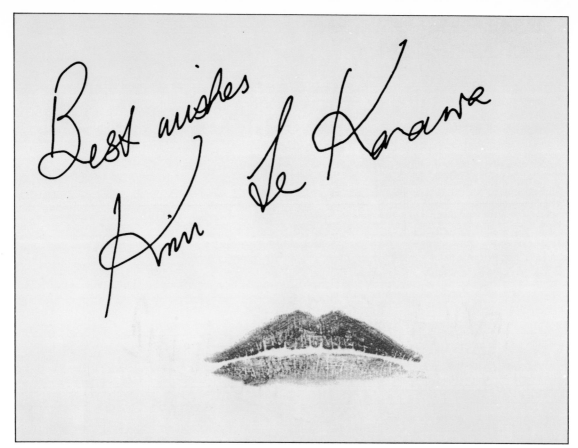

Best wishes

Kiri te Kanawa

Kiri te Kanawa

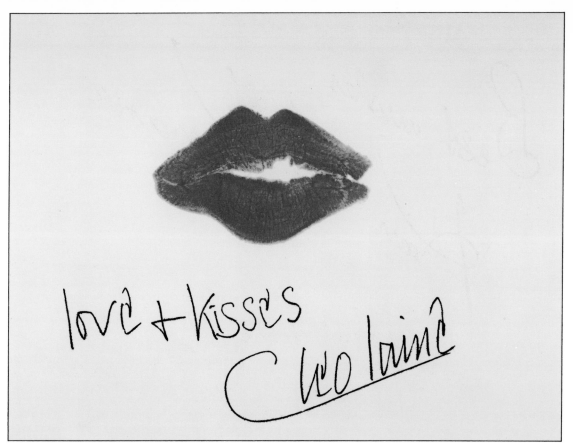

love + kisses
Cleo laine

Cleo Laine

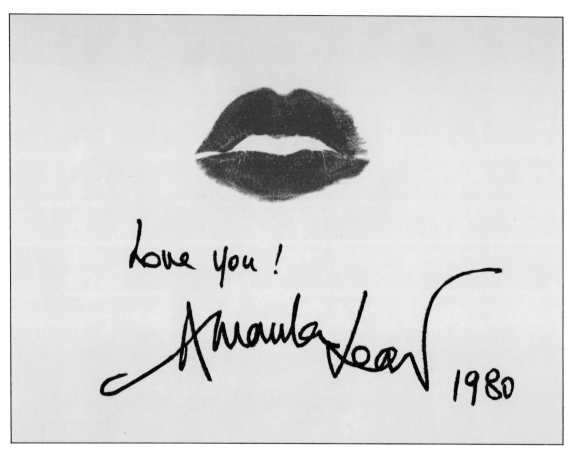

Love you !

Amanda Lear

1980

Amanda Lear

Lord Lichfield

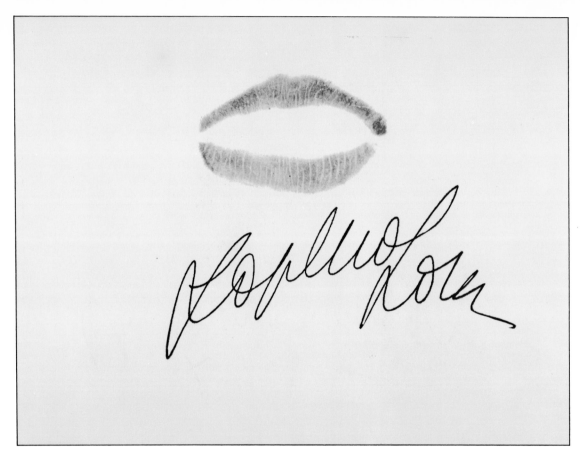

Sophia Loren

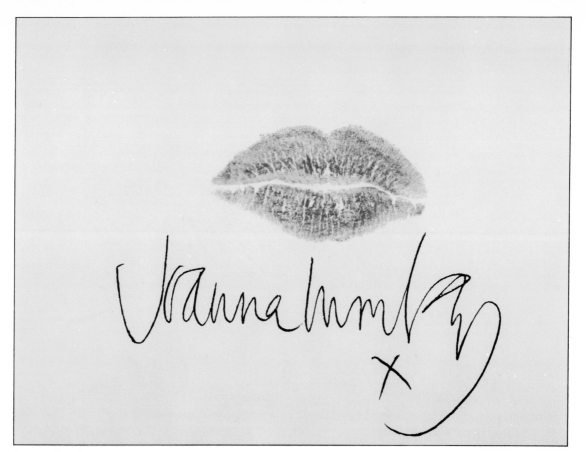

Joanna Lumley

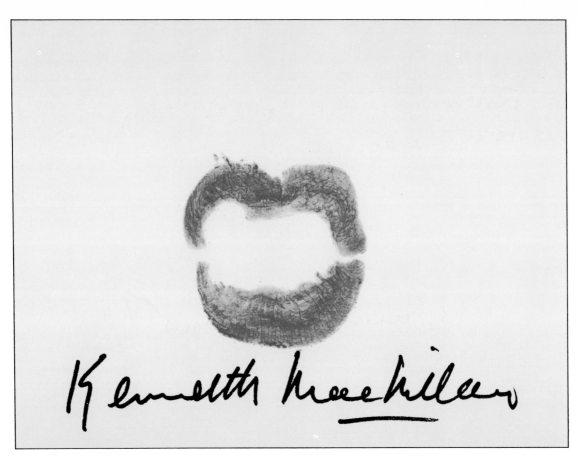

52   Kenneth MacMillan

Rather a smudge, not so easy to Kiss cardboard!

Laura Marlborough

The Duchess of Marlborough

54   Malcolm McDowell

Ian McKellen

love [to] Hills

Hayley Mills

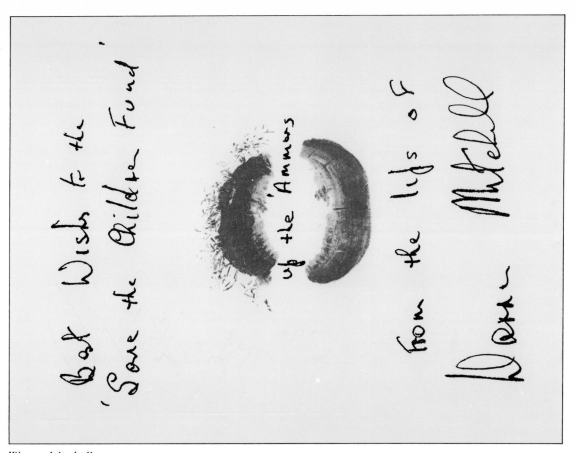

Best Wish to the
'Save the Children Fund'

up the 'Amours

from the lips of

Warren Mitchell

57

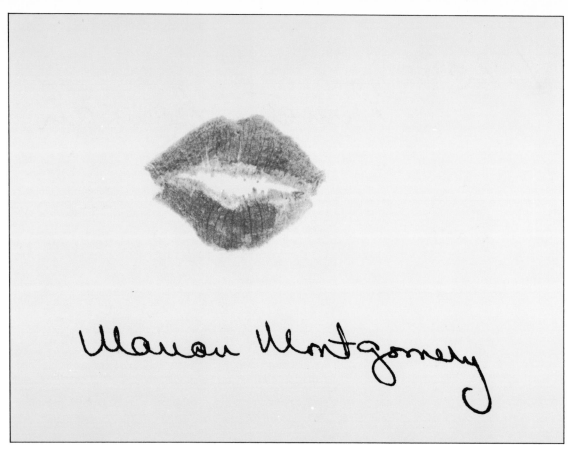

Marian Montgomery

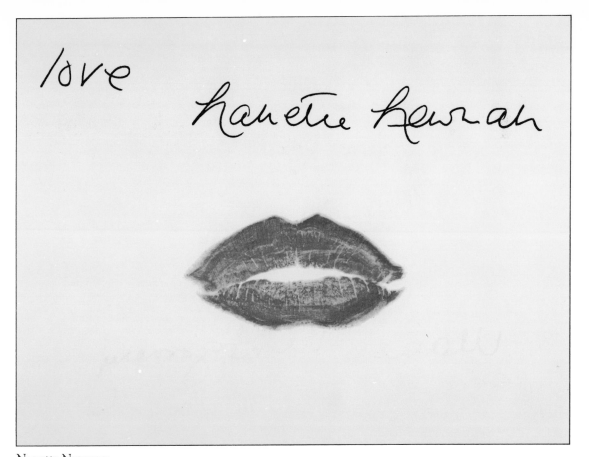

love

nanette newman

Nanette Newman

All the best

Olivia Newton-John
xx

60   Olivia Newton-John

Jack Nicholson

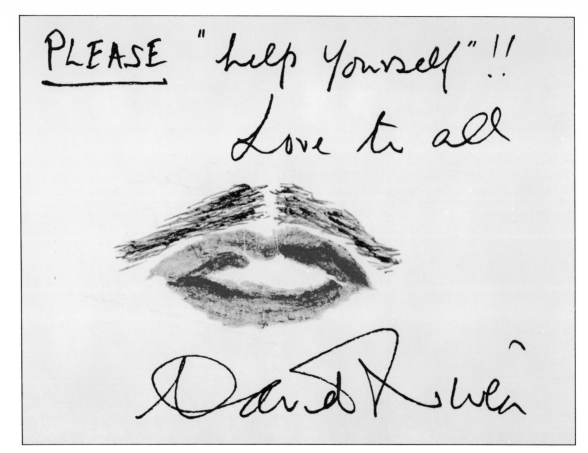

62   David Niven

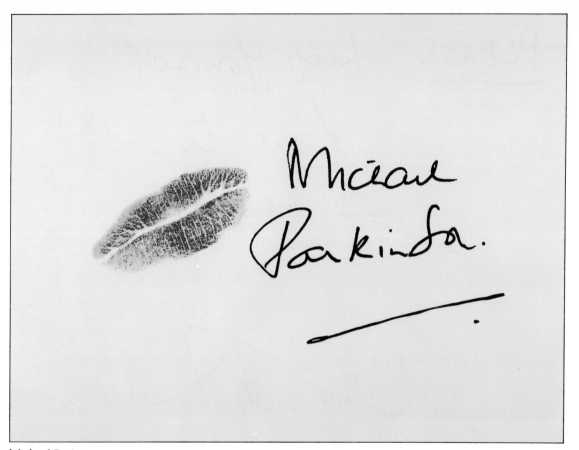

Michael Parkinson

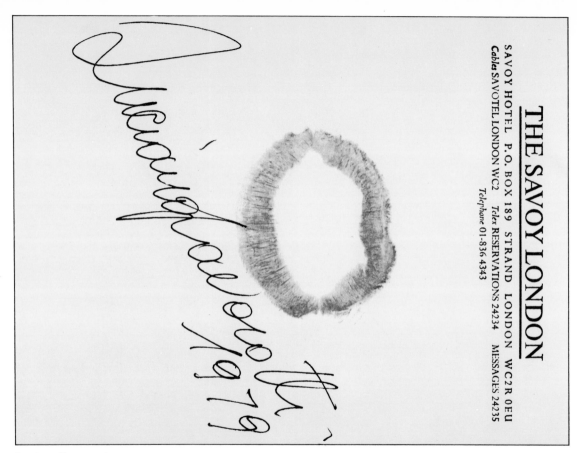

Luciano Pavarotti

Robert Powell

66   Mary Quant

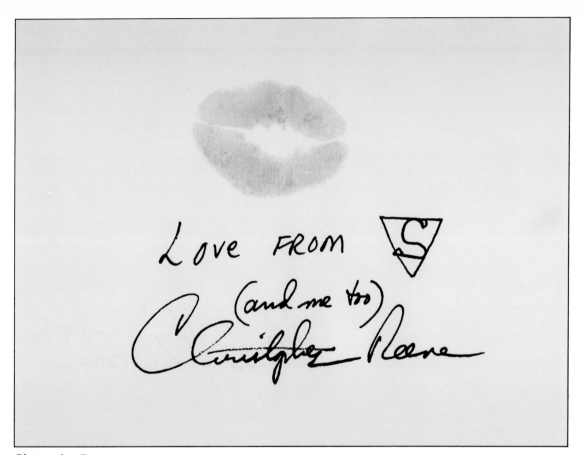

Christopher Reeve

68   Cliff Richard

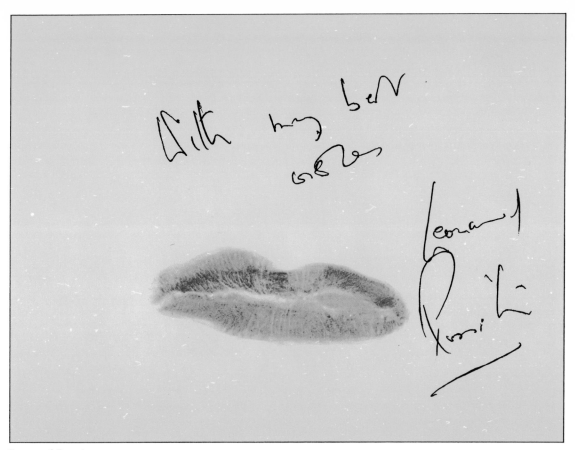

Leonard Rossiter

Omar Sharif

Gerald Scarfe

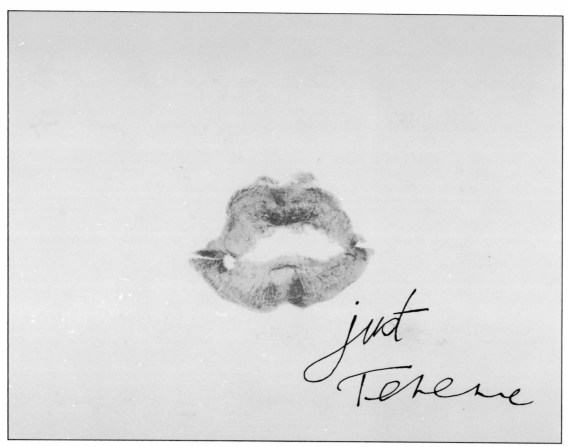

72   Terence Stamp

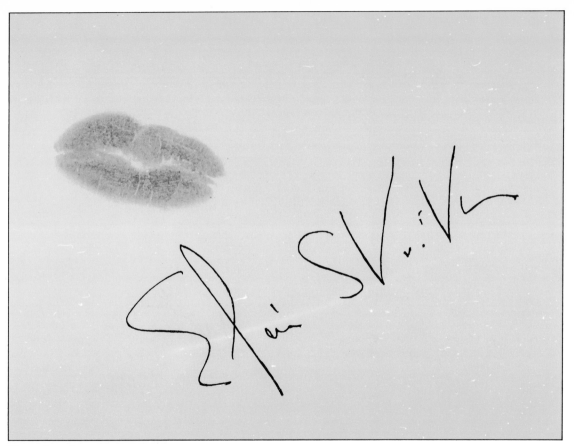

Elaine Stritch

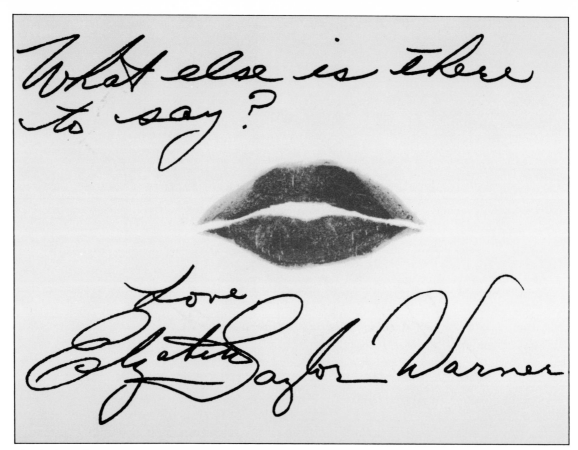

Elizabeth Taylor

John Travolta

The Three Degrees

Peter Ustinov

With lots of love,

Dennis Waterman.

Dennis Waterman

Mae West

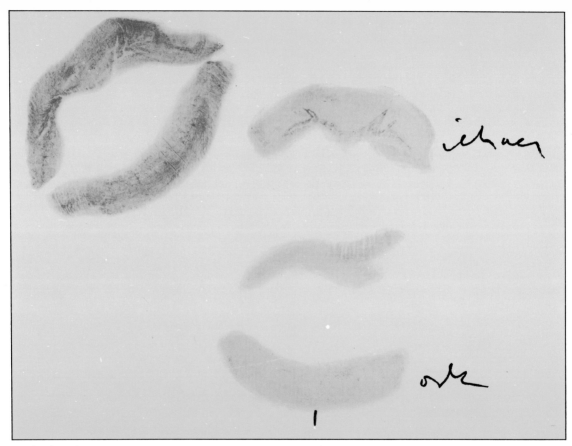

Michael York